50 Spanish Party Recipes for Home

By: Kelly Johnson

Table of Contents

- Patatas Bravas
- Spanish Tortilla
- Gambas al Ajillo (Garlic Shrimp)
- Croquetas de Jamón (Ham Croquettes)
- Albóndigas en Salsa (Meatballs in Tomato Sauce)
- Pimientos de Padrón (Padrón Peppers)
- Pinchos Morunos (Spanish Spiced Skewers)
- Pan con Tomate (Tomato Bread)
- Chorizo a la Sidra (Chorizo in Cider)
- Pulpo a la Gallega (Galician Style Octopus)
- Empanadas Gallegas (Galician Turnovers)
- Boquerones en Vinagre (Marinated Anchovies)
- Ensaladilla Rusa (Russian Salad)
- Espinacas con Garbanzos (Spinach with Chickpeas)
- Bacalao al Pil Pil (Cod in Garlic and Olive Oil Sauce)
- Tostas de Jamón y Tomate (Ham and Tomato Toasts)
- Mejillones a la Marinera (Mariners Mussels)
- Queso Manchego con Membrillo (Manchego Cheese with Quince Paste)
- Champiñones al Ajillo (Garlic Mushrooms)
- Gambas Rebozadas (Battered Prawns)
- Calamares a la Romana (Fried Squid Rings)
- Ensalada de Pulpo (Octopus Salad)
- Espárragos Trigueros a la Plancha (Grilled Wild Asparagus)
- Berenjenas Fritas con Miel (Fried Eggplant with Honey)
- Setas al Ajillo (Garlic Mushrooms)
- Almejas a la Marinera (Mariners Clams)
- Coca de Recapte (Catalan Vegetable Tart)
- Tarta de Santiago (Almond Cake)
- Crema Catalana (Catalan Cream)
- Bunyols de Quaresma (Catalan Lenten Fritters)
- Esqueixada (Catalan Salt Cod Salad)
- Pa Amb Tomaquet (Catalan Tomato Bread)
- Fideuà (Seafood Pasta Paella)
- Escudella i Carn d'Olla (Catalan Meat and Vegetable Soup)
- Panellets (Catalan Almond Sweets)

- Mar i Muntanya (Sea and Mountain Stew)
- Calçots con Romesco (Grilled Spring Onions with Romesco Sauce)
- Crema de Marisco (Seafood Bisque)
- Coca de Recapte (Catalan Vegetable Tart)
- Paella Valenciana (Valencian Paella)
- Tarta de Almendras (Almond Tart)
- Churros con Chocolate (Churros with Hot Chocolate)
- Crema Catalana (Catalan Cream)
- Coca de Sant Joan (Midsummer Catalan Cake)
- Pisto Manchego (Spanish Ratatouille)
- Flan de Huevo (Spanish Creme Caramel)
- Arroz con Leche (Spanish Rice Pudding)
- Bunyols (Spanish Doughnuts)
- Tarta de Queso (Spanish Cheesecake)
- Torrijas (Spanish French Toast)

Patatas Bravas

Ingredients:

- 1 kg (about 2.2 lbs) potatoes, peeled and cut into small cubes
- 3 tablespoons olive oil
- Salt, to taste
- For the Brava Sauce:
    - 2 tablespoons olive oil
    - 2 cloves garlic, minced
    - 1 teaspoon smoked paprika
    - 1/2 teaspoon hot paprika or cayenne pepper (adjust to taste)
    - 1/2 teaspoon ground cumin
    - 1/4 teaspoon ground coriander
    - 1/4 teaspoon ground cinnamon
    - 1/4 teaspoon sugar
    - 1/4 teaspoon salt
    - 1/4 cup tomato sauce
    - 1 tablespoon red wine vinegar
    - 1 tablespoon water

Instructions:

1. Preheat the oven to 200°C (400°F).
2. Place the potato cubes in a large bowl. Drizzle with olive oil and season with salt. Toss until the potatoes are well coated.
3. Spread the potatoes in a single layer on a baking sheet lined with parchment paper. Roast in the preheated oven for about 30-35 minutes or until the potatoes are golden brown and crispy, flipping halfway through cooking.
4. While the potatoes are roasting, prepare the Brava sauce. In a small saucepan, heat the olive oil over medium heat. Add the minced garlic and cook for about 1 minute until fragrant.
5. Stir in the smoked paprika, hot paprika or cayenne pepper, ground cumin, ground coriander, ground cinnamon, sugar, and salt. Cook for another minute, stirring constantly.
6. Add the tomato sauce, red wine vinegar, and water to the saucepan. Stir to combine. Bring the sauce to a simmer and cook for about 5-7 minutes, stirring occasionally, until it thickens slightly. Remove from heat.

7. Once the potatoes are done, transfer them to a serving dish. Drizzle the Brava sauce over the potatoes or serve the sauce on the side for dipping.
8. Garnish with chopped fresh parsley, if desired. Serve hot and enjoy your delicious Patatas Bravas!

Spanish Tortilla

Ingredients:

- 4 large potatoes, peeled and thinly sliced
- 1 large onion, thinly sliced
- 6 eggs
- Salt, to taste
- Olive oil for frying

Instructions:

1. Heat a generous amount of olive oil in a large non-stick skillet over medium heat.
2. Add the sliced potatoes and onions to the skillet. Season with salt to taste. Cook, stirring occasionally, until the potatoes are tender and lightly golden, about 10-15 minutes. Be careful not to let them brown too much.
3. While the potatoes and onions are cooking, crack the eggs into a large mixing bowl. Season with salt and whisk until well beaten.
4. Once the potatoes and onions are cooked, use a slotted spoon to transfer them to the bowl with the beaten eggs. Mix gently to combine, making sure the potatoes and onions are evenly coated with the eggs.
5. Pour off most of the olive oil from the skillet, leaving just a thin coating on the bottom. Return the skillet to the heat.
6. Pour the potato and egg mixture into the skillet, spreading it out evenly with a spatula.
7. Cook the tortilla over medium heat for about 5-7 minutes, or until the bottom is set and lightly golden.
8. To flip the tortilla, place a large plate over the skillet. Carefully invert the skillet so that the tortilla lands on the plate. Then, slide the tortilla back into the skillet to cook the other side.
9. Cook for another 5-7 minutes, or until the tortilla is cooked through and golden on both sides.
10. Once the tortilla is cooked to your liking, transfer it to a serving plate and let it cool slightly before slicing into wedges.
11. Serve the Spanish Tortilla warm or at room temperature, as is traditional, with a side salad or crusty bread. Enjoy your delicious and classic Spanish dish!

Gambas al Ajillo (Garlic Shrimp)

Ingredients:

- 500g (about 1 lb) large shrimp, peeled and deveined
- 6 cloves garlic, thinly sliced
- 1/4 cup olive oil
- 1 teaspoon red pepper flakes (adjust to taste)
- 2 tablespoons chopped fresh parsley
- Salt, to taste
- 1 tablespoon dry white wine (optional)
- Crusty bread, for serving

Instructions:

1. Heat the olive oil in a large skillet over medium heat. Add the sliced garlic and red pepper flakes. Cook, stirring frequently, until the garlic is fragrant and just beginning to turn golden, about 1-2 minutes. Be careful not to let the garlic burn.
2. Add the shrimp to the skillet in a single layer. Season with salt to taste. Cook for 1-2 minutes on each side, or until the shrimp turn pink and opaque. Be careful not to overcook the shrimp, as they can become rubbery.
3. If using white wine, pour it into the skillet and cook for an additional 1-2 minutes, allowing the alcohol to evaporate and the flavors to meld.
4. Remove the skillet from the heat and sprinkle the chopped parsley over the shrimp. Give everything a gentle toss to combine.
5. Serve the Gambas al Ajillo immediately, directly from the skillet, with crusty bread on the side for dipping into the flavorful oil. Enjoy your tasty Spanish garlic shrimp dish!

Croquetas de Jamón (Ham Croquettes)

Ingredients:

- 100g (about 3.5 oz) serrano ham or prosciutto, finely chopped
- 3 tablespoons unsalted butter
- 1/4 cup all-purpose flour
- 1 cup whole milk
- Salt and pepper, to taste
- Pinch of nutmeg (optional)
- 1 egg, beaten
- Fine breadcrumbs, for coating
- Olive oil, for frying

Instructions:

1. In a medium saucepan, melt the butter over medium heat. Add the chopped serrano ham or prosciutto and cook for 2-3 minutes, stirring occasionally, until lightly golden and fragrant.
2. Stir in the flour and cook for another 2 minutes, stirring constantly, to make a roux.
3. Gradually pour in the milk, whisking constantly to prevent lumps from forming. Cook for 5-7 minutes, stirring continuously, until the mixture thickens and becomes smooth and creamy.
4. Season the mixture with salt, pepper, and a pinch of nutmeg, if using. Taste and adjust seasoning as needed.
5. Transfer the mixture to a shallow dish or baking sheet lined with parchment paper. Spread it out evenly and allow it to cool to room temperature.
6. Once the mixture has cooled, cover it with plastic wrap and refrigerate for at least 2 hours, or until firm and chilled.
7. Once chilled, use a spoon or small ice cream scoop to portion out the mixture and shape it into small cylinders or oval-shaped croquettes.
8. Dip each croquette into the beaten egg, then roll it in the breadcrumbs until evenly coated.
9. Heat the olive oil in a large skillet or frying pan over medium heat. Fry the croquettes in batches until golden brown and crispy on all sides, about 2-3 minutes per side.
10. Transfer the cooked croquettes to a plate lined with paper towels to drain any excess oil.

11. Serve the Croquetas de Jamón hot, garnished with fresh parsley or lemon wedges if desired. Enjoy your delicious Spanish ham croquettes as a tasty appetizer or snack!

Albóndigas en Salsa (Meatballs in Tomato Sauce)

Ingredients:

For the meatballs:

- 500g (about 1 lb) ground beef or a mixture of beef and pork
- 1/2 cup breadcrumbs
- 1/4 cup milk
- 1 small onion, finely chopped
- 2 cloves garlic, minced
- 1 egg
- 2 tablespoons chopped fresh parsley
- 1 teaspoon ground cumin
- 1 teaspoon paprika
- Salt and pepper, to taste
- Olive oil, for frying

For the tomato sauce:

- 2 tablespoons olive oil
- 1 onion, finely chopped
- 2 cloves garlic, minced
- 1 can (400g/14 oz) crushed tomatoes
- 1 teaspoon paprika
- 1 teaspoon dried oregano
- Salt and pepper, to taste
- 1/2 cup beef or chicken broth
- Chopped fresh parsley, for garnish (optional)

Instructions:

1. In a large bowl, combine the ground meat, breadcrumbs, milk, chopped onion, minced garlic, egg, chopped parsley, ground cumin, paprika, salt, and pepper. Mix well until everything is evenly combined.
2. Shape the mixture into small meatballs, about 1-1.5 inches in diameter. Place them on a plate or baking sheet lined with parchment paper.
3. Heat a couple of tablespoons of olive oil in a large skillet over medium heat. Add the meatballs in batches and cook until browned on all sides, about 5-7 minutes. Transfer the browned meatballs to a plate and set aside.

4. In the same skillet, add another tablespoon of olive oil if needed. Add the chopped onion and cook until softened, about 3-4 minutes. Add the minced garlic and cook for another minute until fragrant.
5. Stir in the crushed tomatoes, paprika, dried oregano, salt, and pepper. Cook for 5-7 minutes, stirring occasionally, until the sauce thickens slightly.
6. Pour in the beef or chicken broth and stir to combine. Bring the sauce to a simmer.
7. Return the browned meatballs to the skillet, along with any juices that have accumulated on the plate. Spoon some of the tomato sauce over the meatballs to coat them.
8. Cover the skillet with a lid and simmer gently for 15-20 minutes, or until the meatballs are cooked through and tender, and the sauce has thickened.
9. Taste the sauce and adjust the seasoning if needed.
10. Serve the Albóndigas en Salsa hot, garnished with chopped fresh parsley if desired. Enjoy your delicious Spanish meatballs in tomato sauce with crusty bread or over cooked rice!

Pimientos de Padrón (Padrón Peppers)

Ingredients:

- 200g (about 7 oz) Padrón peppers
- 2 tablespoons olive oil
- Sea salt, to taste

Instructions:

1. Rinse the Padrón peppers under cold water and pat them dry with paper towels.
2. Heat the olive oil in a large skillet or frying pan over medium-high heat.
3. Once the oil is hot, add the Padrón peppers to the skillet in a single layer. Be careful, as they may splatter when they hit the hot oil.
4. Fry the peppers for 3-4 minutes, stirring occasionally, until they blister and char slightly on the outside.
5. Use a slotted spoon to transfer the fried peppers to a serving plate lined with paper towels to drain any excess oil.
6. Sprinkle the Pimientos de Padrón with sea salt while they are still hot.
7. Serve the peppers immediately while they are hot and crispy. Enjoy them as a delicious and addictive Spanish appetizer or tapas dish! Remember that the fun of Pimientos de Padrón is the surprise - most are mild, but every so often, you might encounter a spicy one!

Pinchos Morunos (Spanish Spiced Skewers)

Ingredients:

- 200g (about 7 oz) Padrón peppers
- 2 tablespoons olive oil
- Sea salt, to taste

Instructions:

1. Rinse the Padrón peppers under cold water and pat them dry with paper towels.
2. Heat the olive oil in a large skillet or frying pan over medium-high heat.
3. Once the oil is hot, add the Padrón peppers to the skillet in a single layer. Be careful, as they may splatter when they hit the hot oil.
4. Fry the peppers for 3-4 minutes, stirring occasionally, until they blister and char slightly on the outside.
5. Use a slotted spoon to transfer the fried peppers to a serving plate lined with paper towels to drain any excess oil.
6. Sprinkle the Pimientos de Padrón with sea salt while they are still hot.
7. Serve the peppers immediately while they are hot and crispy. Enjoy them as a delicious and addictive Spanish appetizer or tapas dish! Remember that the fun of Pimientos de Padrón is the surprise - most are mild, but every so often, you might encounter a spicy one!

Pan con Tomate (Tomato Bread)

Ingredients:

- Crusty bread (such as baguette or ciabatta), sliced
- Ripe tomatoes (1-2 tomatoes per person)
- 1-2 cloves of garlic, peeled
- Extra virgin olive oil
- Sea salt
- Optional: Serrano ham or anchovies for topping

Instructions:

1. Toast or grill the slices of bread until they are golden brown and crispy on the outside. You can do this in a toaster, on a grill, or in the oven under the broiler.
2. Cut the tomatoes in half crosswise. Take a tomato half and rub it over the surface of each slice of toasted bread, pressing down firmly to release the juices and pulp onto the bread. You want to use the cut side of the tomato to rub over the bread until it's nicely coated with tomato.
3. Once you've rubbed each slice with tomato, discard the remaining tomato skins.
4. Rub each slice of tomato-coated bread with the peeled garlic cloves. The garlic will impart its flavor onto the bread.
5. Drizzle each slice of bread with extra virgin olive oil.
6. Sprinkle a pinch of sea salt over each slice.
7. Optional: Top the Pan con Tomate with slices of Serrano ham or anchovies for extra flavor.
8. Serve the Pan con Tomate immediately as a delicious appetizer or snack. Enjoy the simple and refreshing flavors of ripe tomato, garlic, and olive oil on crispy bread!

Chorizo a la Sidra (Chorizo in Cider)

Ingredients:

- 250g (about 9 oz) Spanish chorizo sausage, sliced into rounds
- 1 cup Spanish apple cider (or any dry cider)
- 2 cloves garlic, minced
- 1 tablespoon olive oil
- Fresh parsley, chopped (for garnish, optional)

Instructions:

1. Heat the olive oil in a large skillet or frying pan over medium heat.
2. Add the sliced chorizo sausage to the skillet and cook for 2-3 minutes on each side, or until lightly browned and crispy.
3. Add the minced garlic to the skillet and cook for another minute, stirring constantly, until fragrant.
4. Pour the apple cider into the skillet, stirring to combine with the chorizo and garlic.
5. Bring the cider to a simmer and cook for 5-7 minutes, or until the cider has reduced slightly and thickened into a sauce.
6. Taste the sauce and adjust the seasoning if needed. Depending on the saltiness of your chorizo, you may not need to add any additional salt.
7. Once the sauce has thickened to your liking, remove the skillet from the heat.
8. Transfer the Chorizo a la Sidra to a serving dish, garnish with chopped fresh parsley if desired, and serve hot. Enjoy your delicious Spanish tapas dish with crusty bread for dipping into the flavorful cider sauce!

Pulpo a la Gallega (Galician Style Octopus)

Ingredients:

- 1 large octopus (about 2-3 kg / 4.5-6.5 lbs), cleaned and thawed if frozen
- 2-3 bay leaves
- Coarse sea salt, for cooking and serving
- Spanish smoked paprika (pimentón), for serving
- Extra virgin olive oil, for serving
- Optional: boiled potatoes, for serving

Instructions:

1. Fill a large pot with water and add the bay leaves. Bring the water to a rolling boil over high heat.
2. Once the water is boiling, carefully lower the octopus into the pot using tongs or a slotted spoon. Make sure the water completely covers the octopus.
3. Reduce the heat to medium-low and simmer the octopus for about 1-1.5 hours, or until it is tender when pierced with a fork or knife. The cooking time will depend on the size and thickness of the octopus, so check for tenderness periodically.
4. Once the octopus is cooked, remove it from the pot and transfer it to a cutting board. Allow it to cool slightly.
5. Cut the octopus into thick slices, about 1/2 to 1 inch thick, using a sharp knife.
6. Arrange the sliced octopus on a serving platter or individual plates.
7. Drizzle the octopus with extra virgin olive oil and sprinkle generously with coarse sea salt and Spanish smoked paprika.
8. Optionally, serve the Pulpo a la Gallega with boiled potatoes on the side.
9. Serve the dish warm, either as an appetizer or as part of a larger meal. Enjoy the tender and flavorful Galician Style Octopus with your favorite crusty bread and a glass of Spanish wine!

Empanadas Gallegas (Galician Turnovers)

For the Dough:

Ingredients:

- 4 cups all-purpose flour
- 1 teaspoon salt
- 1 cup unsalted butter, cold and cut into small cubes
- 1 large egg
- 1/2 cup cold water

Instructions:

1. In a large mixing bowl, combine the flour and salt. Add the cubed butter and use your fingers or a pastry cutter to cut the butter into the flour until the mixture resembles coarse crumbs.
2. In a small bowl, beat the egg with the cold water. Gradually add the egg mixture to the flour mixture, stirring with a fork until the dough comes together. You may not need to use all of the egg mixture.
3. Turn the dough out onto a lightly floured surface and knead it gently until it forms a smooth ball. Wrap the dough in plastic wrap and refrigerate it for at least 30 minutes, or until firm.

For the Filling:

Ingredients:

- 2 tablespoons olive oil
- 1 onion, finely chopped
- 1 red bell pepper, finely chopped
- 1 green bell pepper, finely chopped
- 2 cloves garlic, minced
- 2 cans (about 5 oz each) tuna, drained and flaked (or filling of your choice)
- Salt and pepper, to taste
- 2 hard-boiled eggs, chopped (optional)
- Olives, pitted and chopped (optional)

Instructions:

1. In a large skillet, heat the olive oil over medium heat. Add the chopped onion and bell peppers and cook until softened, about 5-7 minutes.

2. Add the minced garlic to the skillet and cook for another minute until fragrant.
3. Stir in the flaked tuna (or your chosen filling) and cook for 2-3 minutes until heated through. Season with salt and pepper to taste. If using, add the chopped hard-boiled eggs and olives and stir to combine. Remove the skillet from the heat and let the filling cool slightly.

Assembling the Empanadas:

1. Preheat the oven to 375°F (190°C). Line a baking sheet with parchment paper.
2. Divide the chilled dough into two equal portions. Roll out one portion of the dough on a lightly floured surface to about 1/8 inch thickness.
3. Use a round cutter (about 5-6 inches in diameter) to cut out circles of dough. Gather and reroll any scraps as needed.
4. Place a spoonful of the filling in the center of each dough circle. Fold the dough over the filling to form a half-moon shape and press the edges firmly to seal. You can crimp the edges with a fork for decoration, if desired.
5. Repeat the process with the remaining dough and filling.
6. Place the assembled empanadas on the prepared baking sheet. Pierce the tops of the empanadas with a fork to create steam vents.
7. Bake the empanadas in the preheated oven for 20-25 minutes, or until golden brown and crispy.
8. Remove the empanadas from the oven and let them cool slightly before serving. Enjoy your homemade Empanadas Gallegas as a delicious snack or meal!

Boquerones en Vinagre (Marinated Anchovies)

Ingredients:

- 12-16 fresh anchovy fillets, cleaned and deboned
- 1 cup white wine vinegar
- 1/4 cup extra virgin olive oil
- 2 cloves garlic, thinly sliced
- 1 teaspoon coarse sea salt
- 1 teaspoon granulated sugar
- 1/2 teaspoon ground black pepper
- 1/2 teaspoon dried oregano
- 1/2 teaspoon dried thyme
- 1/4 teaspoon red pepper flakes (optional)
- Fresh parsley, chopped (for garnish, optional)

Instructions:

1. Rinse the anchovy fillets under cold water and pat them dry with paper towels. Place the fillets in a shallow dish or glass container.
2. In a small saucepan, combine the white wine vinegar, olive oil, sliced garlic, sea salt, sugar, black pepper, oregano, thyme, and red pepper flakes (if using). Heat the mixture over medium heat just until it starts to simmer. Remove the saucepan from the heat and let the marinade cool slightly.
3. Pour the warm marinade over the anchovy fillets, making sure they are completely submerged. If needed, add more vinegar and olive oil in equal parts to cover the anchovies.
4. Cover the dish or container with plastic wrap or a lid and refrigerate the anchovies for at least 4 hours, or preferably overnight, to allow the flavors to develop.
5. Once marinated, remove the anchovies from the refrigerator and let them come to room temperature before serving.
6. To serve, transfer the anchovies to a serving platter, spooning some of the marinade over the top. Garnish with chopped fresh parsley, if desired.
7. Boquerones en Vinagre can be enjoyed as an appetizer on their own, served with crusty bread or crackers, or as part of a tapas spread. Enjoy the tangy, savory flavor of these marinated anchovies!

Ensaladilla Rusa (Russian Salad)

Ingredients:

- 3 large potatoes, peeled and cut into cubes
- 2 carrots, peeled and diced
- 1 cup frozen peas, thawed
- 3 hard-boiled eggs, chopped
- 1 can (about 5 oz) tuna or cooked ham, drained and flaked
- 1/2 cup pitted olives, sliced
- 1/2 cup mayonnaise
- 2 tablespoons extra virgin olive oil
- 1 tablespoon white wine vinegar or lemon juice
- Salt and pepper, to taste
- Fresh parsley, chopped (for garnish, optional)

Instructions:

1. Place the cubed potatoes and diced carrots in a large pot of salted water. Bring the water to a boil over medium-high heat and cook the potatoes and carrots until they are fork-tender, about 10-12 minutes. Drain and let them cool completely.
2. In a large mixing bowl, combine the cooked potatoes, carrots, thawed peas, chopped hard-boiled eggs, flaked tuna or ham, and sliced olives.
3. In a small bowl, whisk together the mayonnaise, extra virgin olive oil, white wine vinegar or lemon juice, salt, and pepper until smooth and well combined.
4. Pour the dressing over the potato mixture and gently toss until everything is evenly coated.
5. Taste the Ensaladilla Rusa and adjust the seasoning if needed.
6. Transfer the salad to a serving dish and garnish with chopped fresh parsley, if desired.
7. Cover the dish with plastic wrap and refrigerate the Ensaladilla Rusa for at least 1 hour before serving to allow the flavors to meld together.
8. Serve the Russian Salad cold as a side dish or appetizer, accompanied by crusty bread or as part of a tapas spread. Enjoy the creamy and flavorful goodness of this Spanish classic!

Espinacas con Garbanzos (Spinach with Chickpeas)

Ingredients:

- 2 tablespoons olive oil
- 2 cloves garlic, minced
- 1 small onion, finely chopped
- 1 teaspoon ground cumin
- 1 teaspoon smoked paprika
- 1/2 teaspoon red pepper flakes (optional, for heat)
- 1 can (about 15 oz) chickpeas, drained and rinsed
- 1 lb fresh spinach leaves, washed and roughly chopped
- Salt and pepper, to taste
- Lemon wedges, for serving

Instructions:

1. Heat the olive oil in a large skillet or frying pan over medium heat.
2. Add the minced garlic and chopped onion to the skillet and sauté for 2-3 minutes, or until softened and fragrant.
3. Stir in the ground cumin, smoked paprika, and red pepper flakes (if using). Cook for another minute, stirring constantly, to toast the spices.
4. Add the drained chickpeas to the skillet and toss to coat them in the aromatic mixture. Cook for 3-4 minutes to heat through and allow the flavors to meld together.
5. Gradually add the chopped spinach to the skillet, stirring continuously until the spinach wilts down and reduces in volume. This may need to be done in batches depending on the size of your skillet.
6. Once all the spinach has been added, cook for an additional 3-4 minutes, or until the spinach is wilted and tender.
7. Season the Espinacas con Garbanzos with salt and pepper to taste, adjusting the seasoning as needed.
8. Remove the skillet from the heat and transfer the Spinach with Chickpeas to a serving dish.
9. Serve the dish warm, with lemon wedges on the side for squeezing over the top. Enjoy your flavorful and nutritious Espinacas con Garbanzos as a tasty side dish or vegetarian main course!

Bacalao al Pil Pil (Cod in Garlic and Olive Oil Sauce)

Ingredients:

- 4 cod fillets, about 6 ounces each, skin-on
- 1 cup extra virgin olive oil
- 6 cloves garlic, thinly sliced
- 1 dried red

chili pepper, optional

- Salt, to taste
- Chopped fresh parsley, for garnish
- Sliced baguette or crusty bread, for serving

Instructions:

1. Pat the cod fillets dry with paper towels and season them lightly with salt on both sides.
2. In a large skillet, heat the olive oil over medium-low heat. Add the thinly sliced garlic and dried red chili pepper (if using) to the skillet. Cook gently, stirring occasionally, until the garlic becomes golden brown and fragrant. Be careful not to let the garlic burn.
3. Once the garlic is golden brown, increase the heat to medium-high. Carefully add the cod fillets to the skillet, skin-side down.
4. Cook the cod fillets for about 3-4 minutes on each side, or until they are opaque and flake easily with a fork. The cooking time will depend on the thickness of the fillets.
5. As the cod cooks, gently tilt the skillet occasionally to spoon the hot olive oil and garlic sauce over the fillets. This helps to baste the fish and create the creamy emulsified sauce (pil pil).
6. Once the cod is cooked through and the sauce has emulsified, remove the skillet from the heat.
7. Transfer the Bacalao al Pil Pil to serving plates, spooning some of the garlic-infused olive oil sauce over the top.
8. Garnish with chopped fresh parsley and serve immediately, accompanied by sliced baguette or crusty bread to soak up the delicious sauce.

9. Enjoy your flavorful and aromatic Bacalao al Pil Pil as a main course or part of a tapas spread!

Tostas de Jamón y Tomate (Ham and Tomato Toasts)

Ingredients:

- Crusty bread, such as baguette or ciabatta, sliced
- Ripe tomatoes, sliced
- Serrano ham or prosciutto, thinly sliced
- Extra virgin olive oil
- Salt and pepper, to taste
- Optional: Garlic clove, halved (for rubbing the bread)

Instructions:

1. Preheat the oven to 375°F (190°C). Place the slices of bread on a baking sheet and toast them in the preheated oven for 5-7 minutes, or until they are golden brown and crispy. Alternatively, you can toast the bread in a toaster or on a grill.
2. If desired, rub the toasted bread slices with the cut side of a halved garlic clove for extra flavor.
3. Place a slice of ripe tomato on each toast, pressing down gently to release some of the juices onto the bread.
4. Top each toast with a few slices of thinly sliced ham or prosciutto.
5. Drizzle the tostas with extra virgin olive oil and season with salt and pepper to taste.
6. Optional: You can also garnish the tostas with a sprinkle of chopped fresh herbs, such as parsley or basil, for added flavor.
7. Serve the Tostas de Jamón y Tomate immediately as a delicious appetizer or snack. Enjoy the combination of sweet tomatoes, savory ham, and crusty bread with a drizzle of olive oil!

Mejillones a la Marinera (Mariners Mussels)

Ingredients:

- 2 pounds fresh mussels, cleaned and debearded
- 2 tablespoons olive oil
- 1 onion, finely chopped
- 4 cloves garlic, minced
- 1/2 cup white wine
- 1 can (14 oz) crushed tomatoes
- 1 teaspoon paprika
- 1/2 teaspoon dried oregano
- 1/2 teaspoon dried thyme
- Salt and pepper, to taste
- Chopped fresh parsley, for garnish
- Crusty bread, for serving

Instructions:

1. In a large pot or Dutch oven, heat the olive oil over medium heat. Add the chopped onion and minced garlic and sauté until softened and fragrant, about 2-3 minutes.
2. Pour in the white wine and bring it to a simmer. Let it cook for 1-2 minutes to allow the alcohol to evaporate slightly.
3. Stir in the crushed tomatoes, paprika, dried oregano, and dried thyme. Season with salt and pepper to taste. Bring the sauce to a simmer and let it cook for about 10-15 minutes, stirring occasionally, until it thickens slightly and the flavors meld together.
4. While the sauce is simmering, inspect the mussels. Discard any mussels that are open and do not close when tapped, as they may be dead and not safe to eat. Remove any beards attached to the shells.
5. Once the sauce has thickened, add the cleaned mussels to the pot, stirring gently to coat them in the sauce. Cover the pot with a lid and let the mussels steam for 5-7 minutes, or until they have opened.
6. Discard any mussels that have not opened after cooking.
7. Once all the mussels have opened and are cooked through, remove the pot from the heat.

8. Serve the Mejillones a la Marinera hot, garnished with chopped fresh parsley. Serve with crusty bread on the side for soaking up the delicious sauce. Enjoy your flavorful Mariners Mussels as a delightful seafood appetizer or main course!

Queso Manchego con Membrillo (Manchego Cheese with Quince Paste)

Ingredients:

- Manchego cheese, preferably aged (you can choose the level of aging based on your preference)
- Quince paste (also known as membrillo)

Instructions:

1. Start by unwrapping the Manchego cheese from its packaging. Manchego cheese is traditionally made from sheep's milk and has a firm texture with a slightly sharp and nutty flavor.
2. Using a sharp knife, slice the Manchego cheese into thin slices or wedges. You can adjust the thickness of the slices based on your preference.
3. Next, unwrap the quince paste, which is a sweet and tangy jelly-like paste made from quince fruit. Quince paste pairs beautifully with the savory flavor of Manchego cheese.
4. Slice the quince paste into thin slices or cubes that are roughly the same size as the slices of cheese.
5. Arrange the slices of Manchego cheese and quince paste on a serving platter or cheese board. You can alternate the slices of cheese and quince paste or arrange them side by side.
6. Serve the Queso Manchego con Membrillo as a delicious appetizer or part of a cheese platter. The combination of the nutty cheese and sweet quince paste is sure to delight your taste buds!
7. Optionally, you can serve the cheese and quince paste with crackers, bread, or nuts for added texture and flavor contrast.
8. Enjoy this classic Spanish pairing with a glass of wine or your favorite beverage. It's perfect for entertaining guests or as a special treat for yourself!

Champiñones al Ajillo (Garlic Mushrooms)

Ingredients:

- 500g (about 1 lb) mushrooms (button mushrooms or cremini mushrooms work well)
- 4 cloves garlic, thinly sliced
- 1/4 cup extra virgin olive oil
- 1/2 teaspoon chili flakes (adjust to taste, optional)
- Salt and pepper, to taste
- Chopped fresh parsley, for garnish (optional)
- Crusty bread, for serving

Instructions:

1. Clean the mushrooms by wiping them with a damp cloth or paper towel to remove any dirt. Trim the stems if necessary, but you can leave them intact if you prefer.
2. Slice the mushrooms into quarters or thick slices, depending on their size.
3. Heat the olive oil in a large skillet or frying pan over medium heat.
4. Add the sliced garlic to the skillet and cook for 1-2 minutes, stirring frequently, until it becomes fragrant and just begins to turn golden brown. Be careful not to let the garlic burn.
5. Add the sliced mushrooms to the skillet, along with the chili flakes if using. Season with salt and pepper to taste.
6. Cook the mushrooms, stirring occasionally, for 5-7 minutes, or until they are tender and golden brown.
7. Once the mushrooms are cooked, remove the skillet from the heat and transfer the Champiñones al Ajillo to a serving dish.
8. Garnish with chopped fresh parsley if desired.
9. Serve the garlic mushrooms hot, accompanied by crusty bread for dipping into the flavorful olive oil. Enjoy this delicious Spanish tapas dish as an appetizer or side dish!

Gambas Rebozadas (Battered Prawns)

Ingredients:

- 12 large prawns, peeled and deveined, tails left intact
- 1/2 cup all-purpose flour
- 1/2 teaspoon salt
- 1/4 teaspoon black pepper
- 1/4 teaspoon paprika (optional)
- 1 large egg
- 1/2 cup cold sparkling water or beer
- Vegetable oil, for frying
- Lemon wedges, for serving
- Fresh parsley, chopped (for garnish, optional)

Instructions:

1. In a shallow dish, whisk together the flour, salt, black pepper, and paprika (if using) until well combined.
2. In another bowl, beat the egg, then gradually whisk in the cold sparkling water or beer until smooth.
3. Heat vegetable oil in a deep skillet or frying pan over medium-high heat until it reaches 350°F (175°C).
4. While the oil is heating, pat the prawns dry with paper towels to remove any excess moisture.
5. Dip each prawn into the seasoned flour mixture, shaking off any excess.
6. Next, dip the floured prawns into the egg mixture, ensuring they are evenly coated.
7. Carefully place the coated prawns into the hot oil, a few at a time, making sure not to overcrowd the pan.
8. Fry the prawns for 2-3 minutes on each side, or until they are golden brown and crispy.
9. Once cooked, use a slotted spoon to transfer the Gambas Rebozadas to a plate lined with paper towels to drain any excess oil.
10. Repeat the process with the remaining prawns until all are cooked.
11. Serve the Battered Prawns hot, garnished with chopped fresh parsley if desired, and accompanied by lemon wedges for squeezing over the top. Enjoy the crispy and delicious Gambas Rebozadas as a tasty appetizer or snack!

Calamares a la Romana (Fried Squid Rings)

Ingredients:

- 500g (about 1 lb) fresh squid (calamari), cleaned and cut into rings
- 1 cup all-purpose flour
- 1 teaspoon salt
- 1/2 teaspoon black pepper
- 1/2 teaspoon paprika (optional)
- 1/2 cup milk
- Vegetable oil, for frying
- Lemon wedges, for serving
- Aioli or marinara sauce, for dipping (optional)

Instructions:

1. Start by cleaning the squid. Remove the tentacles and discard the innards. Peel off the skin from the body of the squid and discard. Rinse the squid under cold water and pat dry with paper towels. Cut the squid into rings, about 1/2 inch thick.
2. In a shallow dish, whisk together the flour, salt, black pepper, and paprika (if using) until well combined.
3. Pour the milk into another shallow dish.
4. Heat vegetable oil in a deep fryer or large pot to 350°F (175°C).
5. Dip the squid rings into the milk, then dredge them in the seasoned flour mixture, shaking off any excess.
6. Carefully lower the coated squid rings into the hot oil, a few at a time, making sure not to overcrowd the pan. Fry the squid rings for 2-3 minutes, or until they are golden brown and crispy.
7. Use a slotted spoon to transfer the fried squid rings to a plate lined with paper towels to drain any excess oil.
8. Repeat the process with the remaining squid rings until all are cooked.
9. Serve the Calamares a la Romana hot, accompanied by lemon wedges for squeezing over the top. You can also serve them with aioli or marinara sauce for dipping, if desired.
10. Enjoy your crispy and delicious Fried Squid Rings as a tasty appetizer or part of a seafood feast!

Ensalada de Pulpo (Octopus Salad)

Ingredients:

- 500g (about 1 lb) cooked octopus, chilled and sliced into bite-sized pieces
- 1 red onion, thinly sliced
- 1 bell pepper (red, yellow, or green), thinly sliced
- 1 cucumber, thinly sliced
- 2 tomatoes, diced
- 1/4 cup black olives, sliced
- 2 tablespoons chopped fresh parsley
- 2 tablespoons chopped fresh cilantro (optional)
- Juice of 1-2 lemons
- 2 tablespoons extra virgin olive oil
- Salt and pepper, to taste

Instructions:

1. In a large mixing bowl, combine the sliced octopus, red onion, bell pepper, cucumber, diced tomatoes, and sliced black olives.
2. In a small bowl, whisk together the lemon juice and extra virgin olive oil to make the dressing. Season with salt and pepper to taste.
3. Pour the dressing over the octopus and vegetable mixture, tossing gently to coat everything evenly.
4. Sprinkle the chopped fresh parsley (and cilantro, if using) over the top of the salad.
5. Cover the bowl with plastic wrap and refrigerate the Ensalada de Pulpo for at least 30 minutes to allow the flavors to meld together and the salad to chill.
6. Once chilled, give the salad a final toss and taste for seasoning, adjusting as needed.
7. Serve the Octopus Salad cold as a refreshing appetizer or light meal. Enjoy the tender octopus combined with the crisp vegetables and zesty dressing!

Espárragos Trigueros a la Plancha (Grilled Wild Asparagus)

Ingredients:

- 500g (about 1 lb) wild asparagus (espárragos trigueros)
- Extra virgin olive oil
- Coarse sea salt
- Freshly ground black pepper
- Lemon wedges, for serving (optional)

Instructions:

1. Preheat a grill or grill pan over medium-high heat.
2. Trim the tough ends off the wild asparagus spears, if necessary.
3. Drizzle the wild asparagus spears with extra virgin olive oil and season them generously with coarse sea salt and freshly ground black pepper.
4. Place the seasoned asparagus spears on the preheated grill or grill pan in a single layer.
5. Grill the asparagus for 2-3 minutes on each side, or until they are tender and lightly charred, turning them occasionally with tongs.
6. Once the wild asparagus is cooked to your liking, remove them from the grill and transfer them to a serving platter.
7. Serve the Espárragos Trigueros a la Plancha hot, accompanied by lemon wedges for squeezing over the top, if desired.
8. Enjoy the delicious and nutritious grilled wild asparagus as a flavorful side dish or appetizer!

Berenjenas Fritas con Miel (Fried Eggplant with Honey)

Ingredients:

- 1 large eggplant
- Salt
- All-purpose flour, for dredging
- Vegetable oil, for frying
- Honey, for drizzling
- Optional: Ground cinnamon or powdered sugar, for garnish

Instructions:

1. Start by preparing the eggplant. Cut off the stem end and slice the eggplant into thin rounds, about 1/4 inch thick. Place the eggplant slices in a colander and sprinkle them with salt. Let them sit for about 30 minutes to draw out any bitterness and excess moisture. After 30 minutes, rinse the eggplant slices under cold water and pat them dry with paper towels.
2. Heat vegetable oil in a deep skillet or frying pan over medium heat until it reaches about 350°F (175°C).
3. While the oil is heating, dredge the eggplant slices in flour, shaking off any excess.
4. Carefully add the dredged eggplant slices to the hot oil, a few at a time, making sure not to overcrowd the pan. Fry the eggplant slices for 2-3 minutes on each side, or until they are golden brown and crispy. Use a slotted spoon to transfer the fried eggplant slices to a plate lined with paper towels to drain any excess oil.
5. Once all the eggplant slices are fried, arrange them on a serving platter.
6. Drizzle the fried eggplant slices generously with honey.
7. Optionally, sprinkle the Berenjenas Fritas con Miel with ground cinnamon or powdered sugar for added flavor and presentation.
8. Serve the dish immediately as a delicious appetizer or side dish. Enjoy the crispy eggplant slices paired with the sweet honey for a delightful culinary experience!

Setas al Ajillo (Garlic Mushrooms)

Ingredients:

- 500g (about 1 lb) mixed mushrooms (such as button mushrooms, cremini mushrooms, or shiitake mushrooms), cleaned and sliced
- 4 cloves garlic, thinly sliced
- 1/4 cup extra virgin olive oil
- 1/2 teaspoon chili flakes (adjust to taste, optional)
- Salt and pepper, to taste
- Chopped fresh parsley, for garnish (optional)
- Crusty bread, for serving

Instructions:

1. Heat the olive oil in a large skillet or frying pan over medium heat.
2. Add the thinly sliced garlic to the skillet and cook for 1-2 minutes, stirring frequently, until it becomes fragrant and just begins to turn golden brown. Be careful not to let the garlic burn.
3. Add the sliced mushrooms to the skillet, along with the chili flakes if using. Season with salt and pepper to taste.
4. Cook the mushrooms, stirring occasionally, for 5-7 minutes, or until they are tender and golden brown.
5. Once the mushrooms are cooked to your liking, remove the skillet from the heat.
6. Transfer the Setas al Ajillo to a serving dish and garnish with chopped fresh parsley if desired.
7. Serve the Garlic Mushrooms hot, accompanied by crusty bread for soaking up the flavorful olive oil and garlic sauce.
8. Enjoy the Setas al Ajillo as a tasty tapas dish or side dish. The combination of tender mushrooms, garlic, and olive oil is sure to please your taste buds!

Almejas a la Marinera (Mariners Clams)

Ingredients:

- 1 kg (about 2 lbs) fresh clams, scrubbed and cleaned
- 2 tablespoons olive oil
- 4 cloves garlic, minced
- 1 onion, finely chopped
- 1/2 cup white wine
- 1 can (14 oz) crushed tomatoes
- 1 teaspoon paprika
- 1/2 teaspoon dried oregano
- 1/2 teaspoon dried thyme
- Salt and pepper, to taste
- Fresh parsley, chopped (for garnish)
- Crusty bread, for serving

Instructions:

1. Heat the olive oil in a large skillet or pot over medium heat.
2. Add the minced garlic and chopped onion to the skillet and sauté for 2-3 minutes, or until softened and fragrant.
3. Pour in the white wine and bring it to a simmer. Let it cook for 1-2 minutes to allow the alcohol to evaporate slightly.
4. Stir in the crushed tomatoes, paprika, dried oregano, and dried thyme. Season with salt and pepper to taste. Bring the sauce to a simmer and let it cook for about 10-15 minutes, stirring occasionally, until it thickens slightly and the flavors meld together.
5. While the sauce is simmering, inspect the clams. Discard any clams that are cracked or open and do not close when tapped, as they may be dead and not safe to eat.
6. Once the sauce has thickened, add the cleaned clams to the skillet. Cover the skillet with a lid and let the clams steam for 5-7 minutes, or until they have opened. Discard any clams that have not opened after cooking.
7. Once all the clams have opened and are cooked through, remove the skillet from the heat.
8. Serve the Almejas a la Marinera hot, garnished with chopped fresh parsley. Serve with crusty bread on the side for soaking up the delicious sauce.
9. Enjoy your flavorful and aromatic Mariners Clams as a delightful seafood dish!

Coca de Recapte (Catalan Vegetable Tart)

Ingredients:

For the dough:

- 2 cups all-purpose flour
- 1/2 cup warm water
- 1/4 cup olive oil
- 1 teaspoon salt
- 1 teaspoon sugar
- 1 packet (7g) instant yeast

For the topping:

- 2-3 roasted red peppers, peeled and sliced
- 1 onion, thinly sliced
- 1 eggplant, thinly sliced (optional)
- Olive oil, for drizzling
- Salt and pepper, to taste
- Fresh thyme or rosemary, chopped (optional)

Instructions:

1. Preheat your oven to 200°C (400°F).
2. In a large mixing bowl, combine the warm water, sugar, and yeast. Let it sit for 5-10 minutes until foamy.
3. Add the olive oil and salt to the yeast mixture. Gradually add the flour, mixing until a dough forms.
4. Knead the dough on a lightly floured surface for about 5 minutes until smooth and elastic. Shape it into a ball and place it in a lightly oiled bowl. Cover with a clean kitchen towel and let it rise in a warm place for about 1 hour, or until doubled in size.
5. While the dough is rising, prepare the topping ingredients. If using eggplant, you can either grill or roast it until tender.
6. Once the dough has risen, punch it down and transfer it to a lightly floured surface. Roll it out into a large circle or rectangle, about 1/4 inch thick.

7. Transfer the rolled-out dough to a baking sheet lined with parchment paper. Arrange the sliced roasted red peppers, onions, and eggplant (if using) on top of the dough. Drizzle with olive oil and season with salt, pepper, and chopped herbs, if desired.
8. Bake the Coca de Recapte in the preheated oven for 20-25 minutes, or until the crust is golden brown and crispy.
9. Remove from the oven and let it cool slightly before slicing and serving.
10. Enjoy your Coca de Recapte warm or at room temperature as a delicious appetizer, snack, or light meal!

Tarta de Santiago (Almond Cake)

Ingredients:

For the cake:

- 250g (about 2 cups) almond flour
- 200g (about 1 cup) granulated sugar
- 4 large eggs
- Zest of 1 lemon
- Zest of 1 orange
- 1 teaspoon ground cinnamon
- 1/2 teaspoon almond extract (optional)
- Powdered sugar, for dusting

For the topping (optional):

- Blanched whole almonds
- Powdered sugar, for dusting

Instructions:

1. Preheat your oven to 180°C (350°F). Grease and line a 9-inch (23cm) round cake pan with parchment paper.
2. In a large mixing bowl, beat the eggs and granulated sugar together until pale and creamy.
3. Stir in the almond flour, lemon zest, orange zest, ground cinnamon, and almond extract (if using) until well combined. The batter will be thick and sticky.
4. Pour the batter into the prepared cake pan, spreading it out evenly with a spatula.
5. If desired, arrange blanched whole almonds in a decorative pattern on top of the cake.
6. Bake in the preheated oven for 25-30 minutes, or until the cake is golden brown and a toothpick inserted into the center comes out clean.
7. Remove the cake from the oven and let it cool in the pan for 10 minutes before transferring it to a wire rack to cool completely.
8. Once the cake has cooled, dust it with powdered sugar.
9. Serve the Tarta de Santiago sliced and enjoy its delicious almond flavor! It's perfect as a dessert or snack, and it pairs wonderfully with a cup of coffee or tea.

Crema Catalana (Catalan Cream)

Ingredients:

- 4 cups (1 liter) whole milk
- 6 large egg yolks
- 1 cup (200g) granulated sugar
- Zest of 1 lemon
- Zest of 1 orange
- 1 cinnamon stick
- 3 tablespoons cornstarch
- White sugar, for caramelizing

Instructions:

1. In a medium saucepan, combine the milk, lemon zest, orange zest, and cinnamon stick. Heat the mixture over medium heat until it begins to simmer. Remove from heat and let it steep for 15-20 minutes to infuse the flavors.
2. In a mixing bowl, whisk together the egg yolks and granulated sugar until pale and creamy.
3. Remove the cinnamon stick from the milk mixture and discard. Return the saucepan to the stove and heat the milk over medium heat until it reaches a gentle simmer.
4. In a small bowl, mix the cornstarch with a few tablespoons of cold milk to make a slurry. Gradually whisk the cornstarch slurry into the hot milk mixture, stirring constantly, until it thickens slightly.
5. Slowly pour the hot milk mixture into the bowl with the egg yolks and sugar, whisking constantly to temper the eggs.
6. Once combined, pour the mixture back into the saucepan and cook over medium-low heat, stirring constantly, until it thickens to the consistency of custard. This should take about 5-7 minutes. Do not let it boil.
7. Once thickened, remove the custard from heat and strain it through a fine-mesh sieve to remove any lumps or zest.
8. Divide the custard evenly among individual ramekins or serving dishes. Cover each dish with plastic wrap, pressing it directly onto the surface of the custard to prevent a skin from forming. Refrigerate for at least 2-3 hours, or until completely chilled and set.

9. Just before serving, sprinkle a thin, even layer of white sugar over the surface of each custard. Using a kitchen torch, carefully caramelize the sugar until it forms a golden-brown crust.
10. Let the caramelized sugar cool and harden for a few minutes before serving.
11. Serve the Crema Catalana immediately and enjoy its creamy texture and caramelized sugar topping!

Bunyols de Quaresma (Catalan Lenten Fritters)

Ingredients:

- 1 cup (240ml) water
- 1/2 cup (120ml) milk
- 4 tablespoons (55g) unsalted butter
- Zest of 1 lemon
- 1/4 teaspoon salt
- 1 tablespoon sugar
- 1 cup (125g) all-purpose flour
- 4 large eggs
- Vegetable oil, for frying
- Powdered sugar, for dusting

Instructions:

1. In a medium saucepan, combine the water, milk, butter, lemon zest, salt, and sugar. Heat the mixture over medium heat until the butter is melted and the mixture comes to a gentle boil.
2. Reduce the heat to low and add the flour all at once, stirring vigorously with a wooden spoon until the mixture forms a smooth dough and pulls away from the sides of the pan. Continue to cook the dough for an additional 1-2 minutes to cook out the raw flour taste.
3. Remove the dough from the heat and transfer it to a mixing bowl. Let it cool for a few minutes.
4. Once the dough has cooled slightly, add the eggs one at a time, mixing well after each addition. The dough should be smooth and shiny.
5. Heat vegetable oil in a deep skillet or pot to 350°F (175°C).
6. Using two spoons or a small cookie scoop, drop spoonfuls of the dough into the hot oil, working in batches to avoid overcrowding the pan. Fry the bunyols for 3-4 minutes, or until they are puffed up and golden brown, turning them occasionally with a slotted spoon.
7. Once cooked, transfer the bunyols to a plate lined with paper towels to drain any excess oil.
8. Dust the bunyols generously with powdered sugar while they are still warm.
9. Serve the Bunyols de Quaresma warm or at room temperature. Enjoy these delicious Catalan Lenten fritters as a sweet treat during the Lenten season!

Esqueixada (Catalan Salt Cod Salad)

Ingredients:

- 250g (about 9 oz) salt cod (desalted and shredded)
- 2 large ripe tomatoes, diced
- 1 small red onion, thinly sliced
- 1 green bell pepper, thinly sliced
- 1/4 cup black olives, pitted and halved
- 2 tablespoons chopped fresh parsley
- 2 tablespoons olive oil
- 1 tablespoon red wine vinegar
- Salt and pepper, to taste

Instructions:

1. Start by desalting the salt cod. Rinse the cod under cold water to remove any excess salt. Place it in a bowl and cover it with cold water. Let it soak for at least 24 hours in the refrigerator, changing the water 2-3 times during the soaking process.
2. Once the salt cod is desalted, drain it well and shred it into small pieces. Place the shredded cod in a large mixing bowl.
3. Add the diced tomatoes, thinly sliced red onion, thinly sliced green bell pepper, and halved black olives to the bowl with the shredded cod.
4. In a small bowl, whisk together the olive oil and red wine vinegar to make the dressing. Season with salt and pepper to taste.
5. Pour the dressing over the salad ingredients in the mixing bowl. Toss gently to coat everything evenly.
6. Sprinkle the chopped fresh parsley over the top of the salad for added flavor and color.
7. Cover the bowl with plastic wrap and refrigerate the Esqueixada for at least 30 minutes to allow the flavors to meld together.
8. Once chilled, give the salad a final toss and taste for seasoning, adjusting as needed.
9. Serve the Esqueixada cold as a refreshing appetizer or side dish. Enjoy the combination of tender salt cod with the fresh flavors of tomatoes, onions, and bell peppers!

Pa Amb Tomaquet (Catalan Tomato Bread)

Ingredients:

- 1 loaf of rustic bread (such as country bread or baguette), sliced
- 2 ripe tomatoes, halved
- 2 cloves of garlic, peeled
- Extra virgin olive oil
- Coarse sea salt
- Optional: Serrano ham, Manchego cheese, anchovies, or other toppings of your choice

Instructions:

1. Toast the slices of bread until they are golden brown and crisp. You can toast them in a toaster, on a grill, or in the oven.
2. While the bread is still warm, cut one clove of garlic in half and rub the cut side over the surface of each slice of bread. This will infuse the bread with garlic flavor.
3. Cut the ripe tomatoes in half. Rub the cut side of the tomatoes over the surface of each slice of bread, pressing gently to release the juices and pulp. The bread should be well-coated with tomato pulp.
4. Drizzle each slice of bread generously with extra virgin olive oil. Use a good-quality olive oil for the best flavor.
5. Sprinkle a pinch of coarse sea salt over each slice of bread to season it.
6. Serve the Pa Amb Tomaquet immediately as a delicious appetizer or snack. You can enjoy it on its own or top it with additional ingredients such as Serrano ham, Manchego cheese, anchovies, or other toppings of your choice.
7. Enjoy the simple yet flavorful Catalan Tomato Bread as a taste of Catalonia's culinary heritage!

Fideuà (Seafood Pasta Paella)

Ingredients:

- 250g (about 9 oz) fideos (thin vermicelli noodles) or broken spaghetti noodles
- 500g (about 1 lb) mixed seafood (such as shrimp, squid, mussels, and/or clams), cleaned and prepared
- 1 onion, finely chopped
- 2 cloves garlic, minced
- 1 red bell pepper, diced
- 1 ripe tomato, grated
- 1/2 teaspoon smoked paprika
- Pinch of saffron threads (optional)
- 4 cups seafood or chicken broth
- 1/4 cup dry white wine (optional)
- Salt and pepper, to taste
- Olive oil, for cooking
- Lemon wedges, for serving
- Chopped fresh parsley, for garnish

Instructions:

1. Heat a few tablespoons of olive oil in a large skillet or paella pan over medium heat. Add the chopped onion and diced red bell pepper and sauté until softened, about 5 minutes.
2. Add the minced garlic to the pan and cook for another minute, until fragrant.
3. Stir in the grated tomato and smoked paprika. Cook for a few minutes until the tomato has softened and the mixture becomes fragrant.
4. Add the mixed seafood to the pan and cook for a few minutes, until it starts to turn opaque.
5. Stir in the fideos or broken spaghetti noodles, coating them in the mixture.
6. Add the saffron threads (if using) to the seafood or chicken broth to infuse the flavor. Then pour the broth into the pan, along with the white wine (if using). Season with salt and pepper to taste.
7. Bring the mixture to a simmer and cook for about 10-12 minutes, stirring occasionally, until the pasta is cooked and the broth has been absorbed.
8. Once the fideuà is cooked, remove the pan from the heat and let it rest for a few minutes before serving.

9. Serve the Fideuà hot, garnished with chopped fresh parsley and lemon wedges on the side for squeezing over the top.
10. Enjoy this delicious seafood pasta paella as a main course, accompanied by a crisp green salad and crusty bread!

Escudella i Carn d'Olla (Catalan Meat and Vegetable Soup)

Ingredients:

For the broth:

- 1 kg (about 2.2 lbs) beef bones or marrow bones
- 1 kg (about 2.2 lbs) mixed meats (such as beef shank, pork ribs, chicken pieces)
- 2 onions, peeled and halved
- 2 carrots, peeled and chopped
- 2 celery stalks, chopped
- 2 tomatoes, halved
- 2 leeks, cleaned and chopped
- 1 head of garlic, halved
- Handful of parsley
- 2 bay leaves
- Salt, to taste
- Water, to cover

For the soup:

- 200g (about 1 cup) cooked chickpeas (from dried or canned)
- 200g (about 1 cup) cooked white beans (from dried or canned)
- 200g (about 1 cup) cooked pasta (such as small pasta shells or elbow macaroni)
- Salt and pepper, to taste
- Chopped fresh parsley, for garnish
- Crusty bread, for serving

Instructions:

1. Start by making the broth. Place the beef bones and mixed meats in a large stockpot or Dutch oven. Add the onions, carrots, celery, tomatoes, leeks, garlic, parsley, and bay leaves to the pot. Season with salt.
2. Cover the ingredients with water, making sure they are fully submerged. Bring the pot to a boil over high heat, then reduce the heat to low and let it simmer gently for at least 2-3 hours, skimming off any foam and impurities that rise to the surface.

3. After simmering, strain the broth through a fine-mesh sieve or cheesecloth-lined colander into another large pot or bowl. Discard the solids and return the strained broth to the pot.
4. Add the cooked chickpeas, white beans, and pasta to the broth. Bring the soup back to a simmer and let it cook for another 15-20 minutes, or until the pasta is heated through and the flavors have melded together.
5. Season the soup with salt and pepper to taste. Adjust the seasoning as needed.
6. Serve the Escudella i Carn d'Olla hot, garnished with chopped fresh parsley. Serve with crusty bread on the side.
7. Enjoy this comforting Catalan meat and vegetable soup as a hearty meal, especially during the colder months!

Panellets (Catalan Almond Sweets)

Ingredients:

- 250g (about 2 cups) ground almonds
- 200g (about 1 cup) granulated sugar
- Zest of 1 lemon
- 2 large egg yolks
- 1 tablespoon honey
- Pinch of salt
- Pine nuts, for coating
- Optional: Candied fruit or other toppings of your choice

Instructions:

1. Preheat your oven to 180°C (350°F). Line a baking sheet with parchment paper.
2. In a large mixing bowl, combine the ground almonds, granulated sugar, lemon zest, egg yolks, honey, and a pinch of salt. Mix until a dough forms. If the dough is too dry, you can add a little more honey or egg yolk to bind it together.
3. Pinch off small pieces of dough and roll them into balls about 1 inch in diameter.
4. Roll each ball of dough in pine nuts, coating them evenly.
5. Place the coated balls of dough on the prepared baking sheet, leaving some space between them.
6. If using candied fruit or other toppings, gently press them into the tops of the panellets.
7. Bake the panellets in the preheated oven for 12-15 minutes, or until they are golden brown.
8. Remove the panellets from the oven and let them cool completely on the baking sheet.
9. Once cooled, serve the panellets as a sweet treat for All Saints' Day or La Castanyada celebrations.
10. Enjoy these traditional Catalan almond sweets with family and friends, and savor the flavors of this festive tradition!

Mar i Muntanya (Sea and Mountain Stew)

Ingredients:

- 500g (about 1 lb) mixed seafood (such as shrimp, mussels, squid, and/or fish fillets), cleaned and prepared
- 500g (about 1 lb) mixed meat (such as chicken, pork, or rabbit), cut into bite-sized pieces
- 2 onions, finely chopped
- 4 cloves garlic, minced
- 2 tomatoes, diced
- 1 red bell pepper, diced
- 1 green bell pepper, diced
- 200ml (about 3/4 cup) dry white wine
- 2 cups seafood or chicken broth
- 2 bay leaves
- 1 teaspoon smoked paprika
- Pinch of saffron threads (optional)
- Salt and pepper, to taste
- Olive oil, for cooking
- Chopped fresh parsley, for garnish
- Lemon wedges, for serving

Instructions:

1. In a large, deep skillet or Dutch oven, heat a few tablespoons of olive oil over medium-high heat. Add the chopped onions and cook until softened and translucent, about 5 minutes.
2. Add the minced garlic to the skillet and cook for another minute, until fragrant.
3. Add the diced tomatoes, red bell pepper, and green bell pepper to the skillet. Cook for a few minutes until the vegetables start to soften.
4. Push the vegetables to the sides of the skillet and add the mixed meat to the center. Brown the meat on all sides, stirring occasionally.
5. Once the meat is browned, add the mixed seafood to the skillet. Cook for a few minutes until the seafood starts to turn opaque.
6. Deglaze the skillet with the dry white wine, scraping up any browned bits from the bottom of the pan.

7. Stir in the seafood or chicken broth, bay leaves, smoked paprika, and saffron threads (if using). Season with salt and pepper to taste.
8. Bring the mixture to a simmer, then reduce the heat to low. Cover and let it simmer gently for about 20-30 minutes, stirring occasionally, until the meat is cooked through and the flavors have melded together.
9. Once cooked, remove the bay leaves from the skillet.
10. Serve the Mar i Muntanya hot, garnished with chopped fresh parsley and lemon wedges on the side for squeezing over the top.
11. Enjoy this flavorful Catalan Sea and Mountain stew with crusty bread or rice for a satisfying meal!

Calçots con Romesco (Grilled Spring Onions with Romesco Sauce)

Ingredients:

For the Calçots:

- 1 bunch of calçots (large green onions or spring onions)
- Olive oil, for grilling
- Coarse sea salt, for serving

For the Romesco Sauce:

- 2 large roasted red bell peppers, peeled and seeded
- 1/2 cup almonds, toasted
- 1/4 cup hazelnuts, toasted
- 2 cloves garlic
- 2 tablespoons tomato paste
- 2 tablespoons red wine vinegar
- 1 teaspoon smoked paprika
- 1/2 teaspoon cayenne pepper (optional, for added heat)
- 1/4 cup extra virgin olive oil
- Salt and pepper, to taste

Instructions:

1. Preheat your grill to medium-high heat.
2. Trim the root ends and any wilted leaves from the calçots. Leave the green tops intact.
3. Drizzle the calçots with olive oil, tossing to coat them evenly.
4. Place the calçots on the preheated grill and cook for 5-7 minutes on each side, or until they are charred on the outside and tender on the inside. You can also cook them directly on the flames of a gas stove or under a broiler if a grill is not available.
5. While the calçots are grilling, make the Romesco sauce. In a food processor or blender, combine the roasted red bell peppers, toasted almonds, toasted hazelnuts, garlic, tomato paste, red wine vinegar, smoked paprika, and cayenne

pepper (if using). Pulse until the ingredients are finely chopped and well combined.
6. With the food processor or blender running, gradually drizzle in the extra virgin olive oil until the sauce is smooth and creamy. Season with salt and pepper to taste.
7. Once the calçots are cooked, remove them from the grill and transfer them to a serving platter.
8. Serve the grilled calçots with the Romesco sauce on the side for dipping. Sprinkle with coarse sea salt before serving.
9. Enjoy this Catalan delicacy of Grilled Spring Onions with Romesco Sauce as a flavorful appetizer or side dish during your calçotada celebration!

Crema de Marisco (Seafood Bisque)

Ingredients:

- 500g (about 1 lb) mixed seafood (such as shrimp, scallops, mussels, and/or crab meat), cleaned and prepared
- 2 tablespoons olive oil
- 1 onion, finely chopped
- 2 cloves garlic, minced
- 1 carrot, finely chopped
- 1 celery stalk, finely chopped
- 2 tablespoons tomato paste
- 1/4 cup dry white wine
- 4 cups seafood or fish stock
- 1 bay leaf
- 1 teaspoon dried thyme
- 1/2 teaspoon paprika
- 1/2 cup heavy cream
- Salt and pepper, to taste
- Chopped fresh parsley, for garnish
- Crusty bread, for serving

Instructions:

1. Heat the olive oil in a large pot over medium heat. Add the chopped onion, garlic, carrot, and celery. Cook, stirring occasionally, until the vegetables are softened, about 5-7 minutes.
2. Stir in the tomato paste and cook for another minute, until it becomes fragrant.
3. Add the dry white wine to the pot and stir, scraping up any browned bits from the bottom of the pot.
4. Pour in the seafood or fish stock and add the bay leaf, dried thyme, and paprika. Bring the mixture to a simmer and let it cook for about 10 minutes to allow the flavors to meld together.
5. Add the mixed seafood to the pot and cook for a few minutes until the seafood is cooked through. Be careful not to overcook the seafood, as it can become tough.
6. Once the seafood is cooked, remove the pot from the heat. Use a slotted spoon to transfer about half of the seafood to a blender or food processor. Blend until smooth, then return the mixture to the pot.
7. Stir in the heavy cream and season the soup with salt and pepper to taste.

8. Return the pot to the heat and cook for another 2-3 minutes, until the soup is heated through.
9. Serve the Crema de Marisco hot, garnished with chopped fresh parsley. Serve with crusty bread on the side for dipping.
10. Enjoy this delicious and comforting Seafood Bisque as a starter or light meal!

Coca de Recapte (Catalan Vegetable Tart)

Ingredients:

For the pastry:

- 2 cups (250g) all-purpose flour
- 1/2 teaspoon salt
- 1/2 cup (120ml) olive oil
- 1/2 cup (120ml) water

For the topping:

- 2-3 roasted red peppers, sliced
- 1 onion, thinly sliced
- 1 small eggplant, thinly sliced
- 2 tablespoons olive oil
- Salt and pepper, to taste
- Optional: Anchovies, olives, or other toppings of your choice

Instructions:

1. Preheat your oven to 200°C (400°F).
2. In a mixing bowl, combine the flour and salt. Make a well in the center and pour in the olive oil and water. Stir until a dough forms. If the dough is too dry, add a little more water.
3. Transfer the dough to a lightly floured surface and knead it briefly until smooth. Roll it out into a large rectangle or circle, about 1/4 inch thick.
4. Transfer the rolled-out dough to a baking sheet lined with parchment paper.
5. Arrange the sliced roasted red peppers, onions, and eggplant on top of the dough, leaving a border around the edges. Drizzle with olive oil and season with salt and pepper.
6. If using, add anchovies, olives, or any other toppings of your choice.
7. Bake in the preheated oven for 20-25 minutes, or until the crust is golden brown and crisp.
8. Remove from the oven and let it cool slightly before slicing and serving.

9. Enjoy your Coca de Recapte warm or at room temperature as a delicious Catalan vegetable tart!

Paella Valenciana (Valencian Paella)

Ingredients:

- 2 cups Spanish short-grain rice (such as Bomba or Calasparra rice)
- 4 cups chicken or vegetable broth
- 4 bone-in, skin-on chicken thighs, cut in half
- 8 oz rabbit meat, cut into small pieces (optional)
- 1 onion, finely chopped
- 4 cloves garlic, minced
- 1 red bell pepper, sliced
- 1 green bell pepper, sliced
- 1 tomato, grated
- 1 cup green beans, trimmed and halved
- 1 cup artichoke hearts, quartered (fresh or canned)
- 1/2 cup lima beans or broad beans (fresh or frozen)
- 1/2 cup peas (fresh or frozen)
- Pinch of saffron threads
- 1 teaspoon smoked paprika
- Salt and pepper, to taste
- Olive oil, for cooking
- Lemon wedges, for serving

Instructions:

1. Heat the chicken or vegetable broth in a saucepan over medium heat. Once it comes to a simmer, reduce the heat to low to keep it warm.
2. In a large paella pan or skillet, heat a few tablespoons of olive oil over medium-high heat. Season the chicken thighs with salt and pepper, then add them to the pan, skin side down. Cook until golden brown on both sides, about 5-7 minutes per side. Remove from the pan and set aside.
3. If using rabbit meat, add it to the pan and cook until browned on all sides, about 5 minutes. Remove from the pan and set aside.
4. In the same pan, add the chopped onion, garlic, and sliced bell peppers. Cook until softened, about 5 minutes.
5. Stir in the grated tomato, saffron threads, and smoked paprika. Cook for another 2-3 minutes, until the tomato has softened and the mixture is fragrant.
6. Add the rice to the pan and stir to coat it evenly with the vegetable mixture.
7. Arrange the chicken thighs and rabbit meat (if using) on top of the rice.

8. Pour the warm broth into the pan, covering the rice and meat completely. Do not stir the rice after this point.
9. Arrange the green beans, artichoke hearts, lima beans, and peas on top of the rice, distributing them evenly.
10. Cook the paella over medium-low heat, without stirring, for about 20-25 minutes, or until the rice is cooked and most of the liquid has been absorbed. If the rice is still undercooked but the liquid has evaporated, you can add a little more broth and continue cooking until done.
11. Once the rice is cooked, remove the paella from the heat and let it rest for a few minutes before serving.
12. Serve the Paella Valenciana hot, garnished with lemon wedges on the side for squeezing over the top.
13. Enjoy this delicious and authentic Spanish dish with family and friends!

Tarta de Almendras (Almond Tart)

Ingredients:

For the crust:

- 1 1/4 cups (150g) all-purpose flour
- 1/4 cup (50g) granulated sugar
- Pinch of salt
- 1/2 cup (115g) unsalted butter, cold and cubed
- 1 large egg yolk
- 1 tablespoon cold water

For the almond filling:

- 1 cup (100g) almond meal or ground almonds
- 1/2 cup (100g) granulated sugar
- 1/4 cup (60g) unsalted butter, melted
- 2 large eggs
- 1 teaspoon vanilla extract
- Zest of 1 lemon
- 1/4 cup (60ml) milk or cream
- Sliced almonds, for garnish (optional)
- Powdered sugar, for dusting (optional)

Instructions:

1. Preheat your oven to 350°F (180°C). Grease a 9-inch tart pan with a removable bottom.
2. In a large mixing bowl, combine the flour, sugar, and salt for the crust. Add the cold, cubed butter and use your fingers or a pastry cutter to cut the butter into the flour mixture until it resembles coarse crumbs.
3. In a small bowl, whisk together the egg yolk and cold water. Pour the egg mixture into the flour mixture and stir until the dough comes together.
4. Press the dough evenly into the bottom and up the sides of the prepared tart pan. Prick the bottom of the crust with a fork.
5. Bake the crust in the preheated oven for 12-15 minutes, or until lightly golden brown. Remove from the oven and let it cool slightly.

6. While the crust is baking, prepare the almond filling. In a mixing bowl, combine the almond meal, sugar, melted butter, eggs, vanilla extract, lemon zest, and milk or cream. Mix until smooth and well combined.
7. Pour the almond filling into the partially baked tart crust, spreading it out evenly.
8. If desired, sprinkle sliced almonds over the top of the almond filling for garnish.
9. Return the tart to the oven and bake for an additional 25-30 minutes, or until the filling is set and golden brown on top.
10. Remove the tart from the oven and let it cool completely in the pan on a wire rack.
11. Once cooled, remove the tart from the pan and transfer it to a serving platter.
12. Dust the top of the tart with powdered sugar, if desired, before serving.
13. Slice and serve the Almond Tart at room temperature, either plain or with a dollop of whipped cream or a scoop of vanilla ice cream.
14. Enjoy this delicious Spanish dessert with its rich almond flavor and tender, buttery crust!

Churros con Chocolate (Churros with Hot Chocolate)

Ingredients:

For the churros:

- 1 cup water
- 2 tablespoons white sugar
- 1/2 teaspoon salt
- 2 tablespoons vegetable oil
- 1 cup all-purpose flour
- Vegetable oil, for frying

For the cinnamon sugar coating:

- 1/4 cup white sugar
- 1 teaspoon ground cinnamon

For the chocolate dipping sauce:

- 1 cup whole milk
- 100g (about 3.5 oz) dark chocolate, chopped
- 1 tablespoon cornstarch (optional, for thickening)
- Sugar, to taste (optional, for sweetness)
- Pinch of salt

Instructions:

1. In a saucepan, combine the water, sugar, salt, and vegetable oil. Bring the mixture to a boil over medium-high heat.
2. Remove the saucepan from the heat and add the flour all at once. Stir vigorously with a wooden spoon until the mixture forms a smooth dough.
3. Transfer the dough to a piping bag fitted with a star-shaped tip.
4. Heat vegetable oil in a deep skillet or pot to 375°F (190°C).
5. Pipe the dough into the hot oil, using scissors to cut the dough into 4-6 inch lengths as you pipe it. Fry the churros in batches, being careful not to overcrowd the pan, until they are golden brown and crispy, about 2-3 minutes per side.

6. Remove the fried churros from the oil using a slotted spoon and drain them on paper towels to remove excess oil.
7. In a shallow dish, combine the sugar and ground cinnamon for the coating. Roll the warm churros in the cinnamon sugar mixture until coated evenly.
8. To make the chocolate dipping sauce, heat the milk in a saucepan over medium heat until hot but not boiling. Remove from the heat and add the chopped chocolate. Stir until the chocolate is melted and the mixture is smooth. If you prefer a thicker sauce, you can whisk in a tablespoon of cornstarch dissolved in a little cold milk and cook until thickened. Add sugar to taste if desired, along with a pinch of salt.
9. Serve the warm churros with the hot chocolate dipping sauce on the side for dipping.
10. Enjoy the delicious combination of crispy churros and rich chocolate sauce as a delightful Spanish treat!

Crema Catalana (Catalan Cream)

Ingredients:

- 4 cups (1 liter) whole milk
- Zest of 1 lemon
- Zest of 1 orange
- 1 cinnamon stick
- 1 cup (200g) granulated sugar, divided
- 6 large egg yolks
- 1/4 cup (30g) cornstarch
- Additional sugar for caramelizing

Instructions:

1. In a saucepan, combine the whole milk, lemon zest, orange zest, cinnamon stick, and half of the granulated sugar (1/2 cup). Heat the mixture over medium heat until it just begins to simmer, stirring occasionally. Once it simmers, remove it from the heat and let it steep for about 15 minutes to infuse the flavors.
2. In a mixing bowl, whisk together the egg yolks, cornstarch, and the remaining half of the granulated sugar (1/2 cup) until well combined and slightly thickened.
3. After the milk mixture has steeped, remove the cinnamon stick and return the saucepan to the stove. Heat the mixture over medium heat until it just begins to simmer again.
4. Slowly pour a small amount of the hot milk mixture into the egg yolk mixture, whisking constantly, to temper the eggs and prevent them from curdling. Gradually add the rest of the hot milk mixture, whisking continuously until smooth.
5. Return the mixture to the saucepan and cook over medium heat, stirring constantly with a wooden spoon or spatula, until it thickens and coats the back of the spoon, about 5-7 minutes. Be careful not to let it boil.
6. Once the custard has thickened, remove it from the heat and strain it through a fine-mesh sieve into a clean bowl to remove any bits of zest or lumps.
7. Divide the custard evenly among individual serving dishes or ramekins. Cover each dish with plastic wrap, pressing it directly onto the surface of the custard to prevent a skin from forming. Chill the custards in the refrigerator for at least 2 hours, or until set.

8. Before serving, sprinkle a thin, even layer of granulated sugar over the top of each custard. Use a kitchen torch to caramelize the sugar until it melts and forms a golden-brown crust. Alternatively, you can caramelize the sugar under a broiler, watching carefully to prevent burning.
9. Let the caramelized sugar harden for a few minutes before serving.
10. Serve the Crema Catalana immediately, garnished with fresh fruit or mint leaves if desired.
11. Enjoy the creamy, caramelized goodness of this classic Catalan dessert!

Coca de Sant Joan (Midsummer Catalan Cake)

Ingredients:

For the dough:

- 4 cups (500g) all-purpose flour
- 1/2 cup (100g) granulated sugar
- Zest of 1 lemon
- 1/2 teaspoon salt
- 1/2 cup (120ml) warm milk
- 1/2 cup (120ml) warm water
- 1/2 cup (115g) unsalted butter, melted
- 2 large eggs
- 1 packet (7g) active dry yeast

For the filling:

- 1 cup (200g) granulated sugar
- 1 cup (150g) mixed dried fruits (such as raisins, currants, chopped apricots)
- 1/2 cup (75g) chopped nuts (such as almonds, walnuts, or hazelnuts)
- 1/4 cup (60ml) rum or orange juice (optional)
- 1/2 teaspoon ground cinnamon
- Zest of 1 orange
- 1/2 cup (120ml) heavy cream (optional)

Instructions:

1. In a large mixing bowl, combine the warm milk and warm water. Sprinkle the yeast over the liquid and let it sit for 5-10 minutes, until foamy.
2. Add the melted butter, sugar, salt, lemon zest, and eggs to the yeast mixture. Stir until well combined.
3. Gradually add the flour to the wet ingredients, mixing until a soft dough forms. Turn the dough out onto a floured surface and knead for about 5-7 minutes, until smooth and elastic.
4. Place the dough in a greased bowl, cover with a clean kitchen towel or plastic wrap, and let it rise in a warm place for about 1-2 hours, or until doubled in size.

5. While the dough is rising, prepare the filling. In a mixing bowl, combine the granulated sugar, dried fruits, chopped nuts, rum or orange juice (if using), ground cinnamon, and orange zest. Mix until well combined.
6. Preheat your oven to 375°F (190°C). Line a baking sheet with parchment paper.
7. Once the dough has doubled in size, punch it down and divide it into two equal portions. Roll out each portion into a rectangle or oval shape, about 1/4 inch thick.
8. Transfer one piece of rolled-out dough to the prepared baking sheet. Spread the filling evenly over the dough, leaving a border around the edges.
9. If using, pour the heavy cream over the filling.
10. Place the second piece of rolled-out dough over the filling, pressing down gently around the edges to seal.
11. Use a sharp knife to make diagonal cuts across the top layer of dough, creating a diamond pattern.
12. Bake the Coca de Sant Joan in the preheated oven for 25-30 minutes, or until golden brown and cooked through.
13. Remove from the oven and let it cool slightly before serving.
14. Serve the Coca de Sant Joan warm or at room temperature, sliced into squares or wedges.
15. Enjoy this delicious Catalan cake as part of your Sant Joan celebration!

Pisto Manchego (Spanish Ratatouille)

Ingredients:

- 2 tablespoons olive oil
- 1 onion, finely chopped
- 2 cloves garlic, minced
- 1 red bell pepper, diced
- 1 green bell pepper, diced
- 1 eggplant, diced
- 2 zucchini, diced
- 4 ripe tomatoes, peeled and diced
- 1 teaspoon smoked paprika
- Salt and pepper, to taste
- Chopped fresh parsley or basil, for garnish (optional)

Instructions:

1. Heat the olive oil in a large skillet or Dutch oven over medium heat.
2. Add the chopped onion and minced garlic to the skillet. Cook, stirring occasionally, until the onion is softened and translucent, about 5 minutes.
3. Add the diced red and green bell peppers to the skillet. Cook for another 5 minutes, until the peppers begin to soften.
4. Stir in the diced eggplant and zucchini. Cook for 8-10 minutes, stirring occasionally, until the vegetables are tender.
5. Add the diced tomatoes to the skillet, along with the smoked paprika, salt, and pepper. Stir to combine.
6. Reduce the heat to low and let the mixture simmer gently for 15-20 minutes, allowing the flavors to meld together and the liquid to reduce slightly. If the mixture becomes too dry, you can add a splash of water or vegetable broth.
7. Taste and adjust the seasoning, adding more salt and pepper if needed.
8. Once the vegetables are tender and the flavors have developed, remove the skillet from the heat.
9. Serve the Pisto Manchego hot, garnished with chopped fresh parsley or basil if desired.
10. Enjoy this flavorful Spanish ratatouille as a vegetarian main dish, side dish, or even as a filling for omelets or sandwiches!

Flan de Huevo (Spanish Creme Caramel)

Ingredients:

For the caramel:

- 1 cup (200g) granulated sugar
- 1/4 cup (60ml) water

For the custard:

- 4 large eggs
- 1 can (14 oz / 400ml) sweetened condensed milk
- 1 can (12 oz / 354ml) evaporated milk
- 1 teaspoon vanilla extract

Instructions:

1. Preheat your oven to 350°F (175°C). Place a roasting pan filled with about 1 inch of hot water in the oven to create a water bath for baking the flan.
2. To make the caramel, place the granulated sugar and water in a small saucepan. Cook over medium heat, stirring occasionally, until the sugar has dissolved.
3. Once the sugar has dissolved, stop stirring and let the mixture come to a simmer. Cook, without stirring, until the mixture turns a deep amber color, about 5-7 minutes. Swirl the pan occasionally to ensure even caramelization.
4. Once the caramel reaches the desired color, immediately pour it into the bottom of a 9-inch round cake pan or flan mold, swirling to coat the bottom evenly. Be careful, as the caramel will be very hot. Quickly tilt the pan to coat the sides with caramel as well.
5. In a mixing bowl, whisk together the eggs, sweetened condensed milk, evaporated milk, and vanilla extract until smooth and well combined.
6. Pour the custard mixture over the caramel in the cake pan or flan mold.
7. Carefully transfer the cake pan or flan mold to the preheated oven, placing it in the roasting pan filled with hot water to create a water bath.
8. Bake the flan in the water bath for 50-60 minutes, or until the custard is set around the edges but still slightly jiggly in the center.
9. Once the flan is done baking, remove it from the oven and let it cool to room temperature.

10. Once cooled, cover the flan with plastic wrap and refrigerate for at least 4 hours, or preferably overnight, to chill and set completely.
11. To serve, run a knife around the edges of the flan to loosen it from the pan. Place a serving plate upside down on top of the pan, then quickly and carefully invert the flan onto the plate. The caramel sauce will flow over the top of the flan.
12. Slice and serve the Flan de Huevo chilled, with the caramel sauce drizzled over the top.
13. Enjoy this delicious and creamy Spanish Creme Caramel as a delightful dessert!

Arroz con Leche (Spanish Rice Pudding)

Ingredients:

- 1 cup (200g) white rice (short or medium-grain)
- 4 cups (1 liter) whole milk
- 1 cinnamon stick
- Zest of 1 lemon
- 1/2 cup (100g) granulated sugar
- Pinch of salt
- 1 teaspoon vanilla extract
- Ground cinnamon, for garnish (optional)
- Raisins or chopped nuts, for garnish (optional)

Instructions:

1. Rinse the rice under cold water until the water runs clear. This helps remove excess starch from the rice.
2. In a large saucepan, combine the rinsed rice, whole milk, cinnamon stick, and lemon zest. Bring the mixture to a simmer over medium heat, stirring occasionally to prevent the rice from sticking to the bottom of the pan.
3. Once the mixture comes to a simmer, reduce the heat to low and let it simmer gently, stirring occasionally, for about 30-40 minutes, or until the rice is tender and the mixture has thickened to your desired consistency. Be sure to scrape the bottom of the pan to prevent the rice from sticking.
4. Stir in the granulated sugar, salt, and vanilla extract. Continue to cook for another 5-10 minutes, stirring constantly, until the sugar has dissolved and the mixture is smooth and creamy.
5. Once the rice pudding has reached your desired consistency, remove the saucepan from the heat and discard the cinnamon stick and lemon zest.
6. Transfer the rice pudding to individual serving bowls or a large serving dish. Let it cool slightly before serving, or refrigerate it for a few hours to serve chilled.
7. If desired, sprinkle ground cinnamon over the top of the rice pudding for garnish.
8. Serve the Arroz con Leche warm or chilled, garnished with raisins or chopped nuts if desired.
9. Enjoy this comforting and delicious Spanish Rice Pudding as a sweet ending to any meal or as a comforting treat on its own!

Bunyols (Spanish Doughnuts)

Ingredients:

- 1 cup (240ml) water
- 4 tablespoons (56g) unsalted butter
- 1/2 teaspoon salt
- 1 cup (125g) all-purpose flour
- 4 large eggs
- Vegetable oil, for frying
- Granulated sugar, for dusting

Instructions:

1. In a medium saucepan, combine water, butter, and salt. Bring to a boil over medium heat.
2. Reduce heat to low and add flour all at once. Stir vigorously with a wooden spoon until the mixture forms a smooth dough and pulls away from the sides of the pan.
3. Remove from heat and let cool for a few minutes.
4. Add eggs one at a time, mixing well after each addition, until you have a smooth, thick batter.
5. Heat vegetable oil in a deep skillet or pot to 350°F (175°C).
6. Once the oil is hot, drop spoonfuls of batter into the oil, frying in batches. Be careful not to overcrowd the pot.
7. Fry the bunyols until they are golden brown and crispy, about 2-3 minutes per side.
8. Remove from the oil using a slotted spoon and drain on paper towels to remove excess oil.
9. While still warm, roll the bunyols in granulated sugar to coat evenly.
10. Serve immediately as a delicious snack or dessert.

Enjoy these crispy and sweet Spanish doughnuts! You can also experiment with different flavors or fillings, such as adding lemon zest or filling them with pastry cream or chocolate.

Tarta de Queso (Spanish Cheesecake)

Ingredients:

For the crust:

- 200g (about 7 oz) digestive biscuits or graham crackers
- 100g (about 7 tablespoons) unsalted butter, melted

For the cheesecake filling:

- 500g (about 18 oz) cream cheese, at room temperature
- 200g (about 1 cup) granulated sugar
- 4 large eggs, at room temperature
- Zest of 1 lemon (optional)
- 1 teaspoon vanilla extract
- 200ml (about 3/4 cup) heavy cream
- 2 tablespoons all-purpose flour
- Pinch of salt

Instructions:

1. Preheat your oven to 325°F (160°C). Grease a 9-inch (23cm) springform pan and line the bottom with parchment paper.
2. Crush the digestive biscuits or graham crackers into fine crumbs. You can do this by placing them in a plastic bag and crushing them with a rolling pin, or by using a food processor.
3. In a mixing bowl, combine the biscuit crumbs with the melted butter until well combined. Press the mixture into the bottom of the prepared springform pan, using the back of a spoon or your fingers to create an even layer. Refrigerate while you prepare the filling.
4. In a large mixing bowl, beat the cream cheese and sugar together until smooth and creamy.
5. Add the eggs one at a time, beating well after each addition. Add the lemon zest (if using) and vanilla extract, and beat until incorporated.

6. In a separate small bowl, whisk together the heavy cream, flour, and salt until smooth. Gradually add this mixture to the cream cheese mixture, beating until well combined and smooth.
7. Pour the cheesecake filling over the chilled crust in the springform pan, smoothing the top with a spatula.
8. Bake the cheesecake in the preheated oven for 45-55 minutes, or until the edges are set and the center is slightly wobbly.
9. Turn off the oven and leave the cheesecake inside with the door slightly ajar for about 1 hour to cool gradually.
10. Remove the cheesecake from the oven and let it cool completely at room temperature. Then refrigerate for at least 4 hours, or preferably overnight, to chill and set completely.
11. Once chilled, carefully remove the cheesecake from the springform pan. Slice and serve chilled.
12. Enjoy this creamy and delicious Spanish cheesecake as a delightful dessert!

Feel free to garnish your Tarta de Queso with fresh berries, fruit compote, or a drizzle of caramel sauce for added flavor and presentation.

Torrijas (Spanish French Toast)

Ingredients:

- 1 loaf of stale bread (preferably a dense bread like brioche or baguette), sliced into thick slices
- 4 cups (1 liter) whole milk
- 1 cinnamon stick
- Zest of 1 lemon
- 4 large eggs
- 1/2 cup (100g) granulated sugar, plus more for sprinkling
- Vegetable oil, for frying
- Ground cinnamon, for dusting (optional)
- Honey, for drizzling (optional)

Instructions:

1. In a large saucepan, combine the whole milk, cinnamon stick, and lemon zest. Heat over medium heat until the mixture is warm but not boiling. Remove from heat and let cool slightly.
2. In a shallow dish, whisk together the eggs and granulated sugar until well combined.
3. Dip each slice of bread into the milk mixture, soaking it for about 10-15 seconds on each side. Be sure the bread is thoroughly soaked but not falling apart.
4. Heat vegetable oil in a large skillet or frying pan over medium heat.
5. Carefully transfer the soaked bread slices to the hot skillet. Fry them in batches, being careful not to overcrowd the pan, until they are golden brown and crispy on both sides, about 2-3 minutes per side.
6. Once fried, transfer the torrijas to a plate lined with paper towels to drain excess oil.
7. While still warm, sprinkle the torrijas with granulated sugar and ground cinnamon, if desired.
8. Serve the torrijas warm, drizzled with honey if desired.
9. Enjoy these delicious Spanish French toast as a sweet and comforting dessert or breakfast treat!

Torrijas can be enjoyed warm or at room temperature. They are often served as is, but you can also accompany them with a dollop of whipped cream, a scoop of vanilla ice cream, or a sprinkle of powdered sugar for added sweetness.